Baby

Practical wisdom from one mother to another

Jennifer L. Cowart

March 12, 2011

To Jay + Karen —

Best Wishes!

Jennifer L Cowart

Heart & Soul Publishing

Baby Notes:
Practical Wisdom from One Mother to Another

Copyright © 2011 by Jennifer L. Cowart

ALL RIGHTS RESERVED.

No part of this book shall be reproduced or transmitted in any form by any mechanical, photographic or electronic process, including photocopying and recording, or by any information storage and retrieval system, except as may be expressly permitted by the publisher. The scanning, uploading and distribution of this book on the internet or by other means without permission of the publisher is illegal and punishable by law. Please purchase only authorized electronic editions. Your support of the author's rights is appreciated.

ISBN: 978-0-9827229-1-6

Published and distributed by Heart & Soul Publishing

Printed in the USA

Cover and interior design: David Aldrich

For Information Contact:

Heart & Soul Publishing
Telephone: (401)383-6062
Email: HeartandSoulPublishing@gmail.com

Visit us at www.HeartandSoulPublishing.com

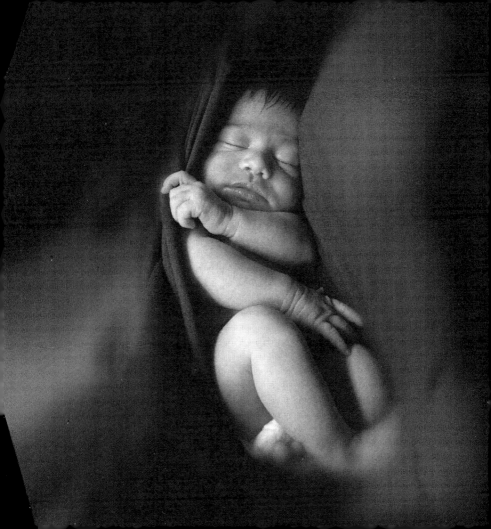

*For my husband and my three daughters.
Without you I would not be the mother
that I am today.*

Introduction
The story behind the story

They say motherhood is the toughest job you will ever love and that it is the most rewarding job you will ever have. What they don't tell you is just how tough it can be at times. Mixed in with all of the wonder, excitement and joy are times of uncertainty, guilt and frustration.

When my brother and his wife were expecting their first baby in 2009, I tried to think of my best motherhood advice to give them. I had given birth to my first daughter ten years prior, and had gone on to have two more daughters over the years.

As I sat one night just before their baby shower, I tried to think of all I had learned up to that point about having babies and kids. I wrote down everything I could think of that I wanted to pass on to them. I called it "Important Notes," and I made it into a cute little handmade booklet for them. I sent it off to them with their gift, and I didn't even keep a duplicate list for myself.

Upon visiting them for their daughter's first birthday a year later, my sister-in-law mentioned the "Important Notes," and how she had been looking through it again recently. I asked her if she wouldn't mind sending me a copy of the list to keep, since several of my friends had recently had babies.

When the list arrived in my email inbox I decided to share it with some of my friends through a social networking site. The response was overwhelming. Many of my friends wrote to me, asking if they could share my list with their daughters, granddaughters and nieces. The list had made them laugh and cry. They were happy to hear that other mothers felt the way they did, that they weren't alone in the newness of motherhood.

I decided to make the list into an actual book, changing the title slightly, so that I could share it with mothers everywhere. I am not a doctor. I am not a psychologist, and I'm certainly not an expert. What I am is an experienced, hands-on mom. I've been through pregnancy, childbirth and child-rearing three times over. I know everyone's philosophies and experiences are different, and I know

I still have the teenage years and beyond to get through, but I do believe that there is a common thread connecting mothers everywhere. I believe that if we all share our experiences and our wisdom, our paths will be made just a little bit easier as we travel down the road of parenthood.

I have included several blank pages at the end of this book for you to add your own wisdom, whether it's something you've come up with on your own or something that has been shared with you. You might find that someday you can pass your wisdom on to another mother and make her path a little bit easier to travel as well.

Congratulations and best wishes to you all,

Jennifer Cowart

Acknowledgements

I have so many people to thank. To all of the moms, including my own mom and my mother-in-law, all of whom have cared enough to share their tips with me during the last eleven years as I have raised and continue to raise my own children, I thank you. I especially want to thank Karen, Inga, Marcia and Stacey for their tips. It is everyone's wisdom, mixed in with my own, that I share with you in *Baby Notes*.

I also want to thank the Cerbo, Morello, Camelo, Minicucci, DeRouin, Goldthwait, Schiff, Voccio, Vose, Wandyes, and Waterman families, all of whom have shared their baby photos with me for use in this book. Your photos have truly brought my words to life.

I want to thank my entire family for encouraging me and supporting me throughout this process, especially my parents, and my wonderful husband Don. He has been right there beside me through these first eleven years of parenting.

I would like to thank David and Jayne DeRouin of Heart & Soul Publishing and Dave Aldrich of Aldrich Design. David and Jayne have made the publishing of this book possible, and gave me the confidence I needed to believe in this project. It was Dave Aldrich's design talents that transformed my vision for *Baby Notes* into this gorgeous book.

Finally, I would be remiss if I didn't thank my brother Chris and my sister-in-law Nina, for being the people who inspired me to create the original "Important Notes," in 2009. As this book goes to print in 2011 they have just welcomed their second baby, James, into the world. The ultrasound photo at the end of this book is of James, and their daughter Maya is the baby on the cover, which is only fitting.

Without all of you, this book would not be possible.

My most sincere love and thanks
to everyone,

Jen

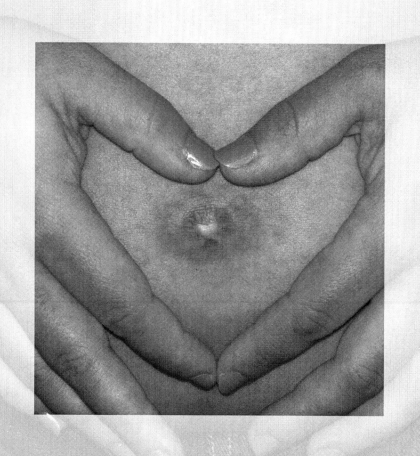

When you are pregnant it seems you can't remember when you weren't.

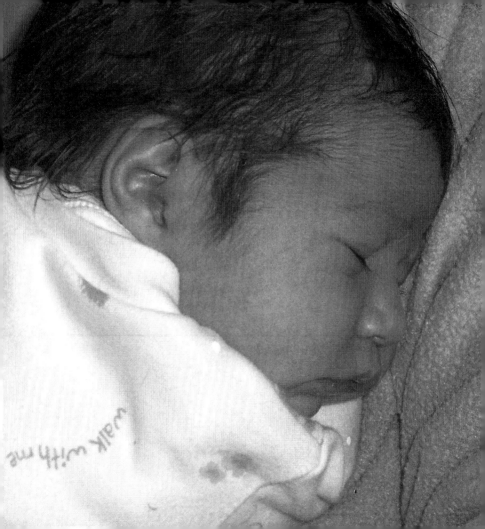

When the baby arrives, you can't remember being pregnant.

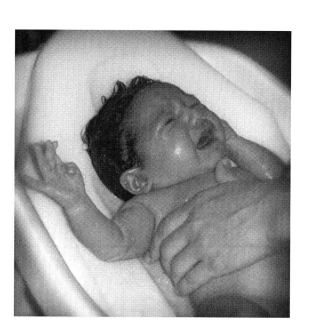

*The first few weeks are the hardest,
but it does get easier.*

*Your house won't be perfect.
You won't get everything done.
Don't be afraid to let some things go.*

In the beginning, it takes an entire day to do something as simple as emptying the dishwasher or taking a shower.

Later on, they can shower themselves, as well as each other, while you empty the dishwasher.

Life will be a bit crazy and disorganized. Have plenty of snacks on hand and some pre-made meals ready and frozen for those crazy nights.

Don't be afraid to ask for help. Find a good network of other new moms and dads to bounce things off of.

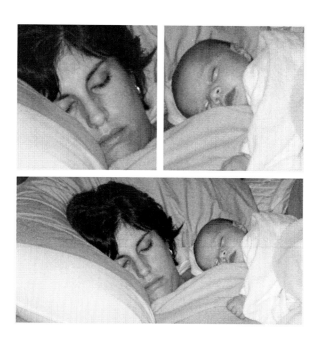

For the most part, unless you have your kids really close together, the first baby is the only one where you can "sleep when the baby sleeps" - - so be sure you do.

Don't be afraid to let Daddy be the favorite. That way, when they are crying in the middle of the night, they cry for Daddy, and Mommy can stay in bed.

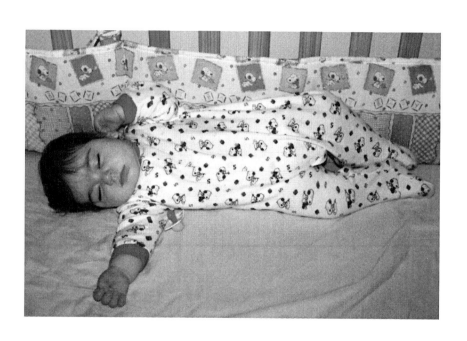

*When you lay awake at night,
waiting for them to wake up, they don't.*

*When you desperately
need them to sleep, they won't.*

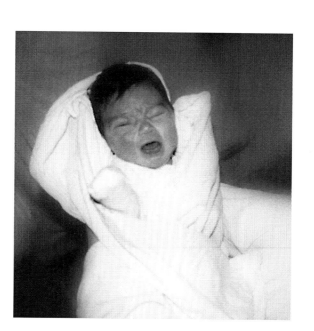

No matter how late you keep them up at night, they still wake up at the same time each morning; they're just crankier because now they've lost sleep.

Never wake a sleeping baby.
If you do accidentally wake them,
never make eye contact!

Skipping a nap is (almost) never worth it.

*Just when you think you can't
take it anymore, it stops.*

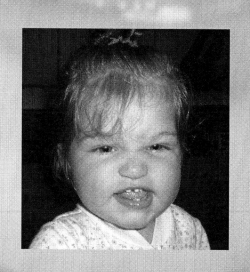

*Just when you think you've
got it figured out, teeth come in.*

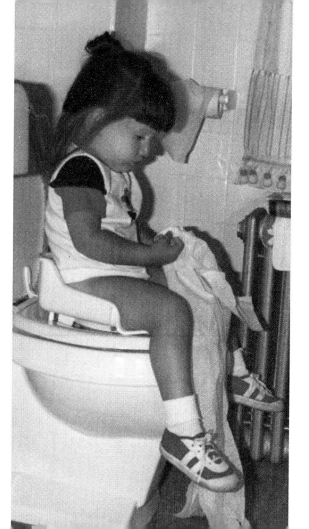

Although when you're in the middle of it, it seems awful, you will look back on it later and laugh (or at least give a little smile.)

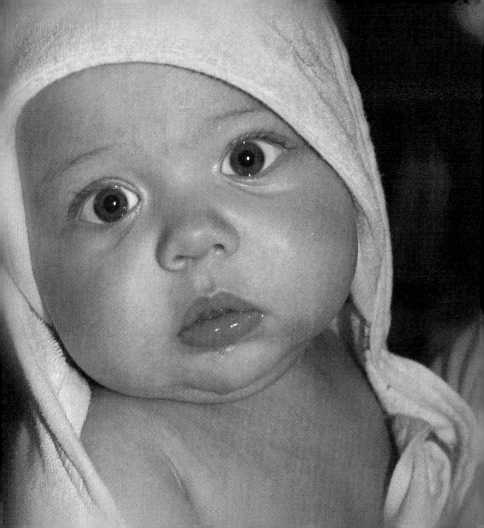

Babies are resilient.

Babies are forgiving.

Mother's guilt is torturous.

*Fathers don't have any guilt.**

This one isn't exactly true, but it's been my experience that fathers don't have nearly as much guilt as mothers do. Mothers have guilt over every little thing and it lasts a long time. Fathers tend to ration their guilt, using it only when absolutely necessary.

No one hears if you cry in the shower.

Each day is a new beginning.

*Usually if you're at a crossroads,
the hard answer is the best one.*

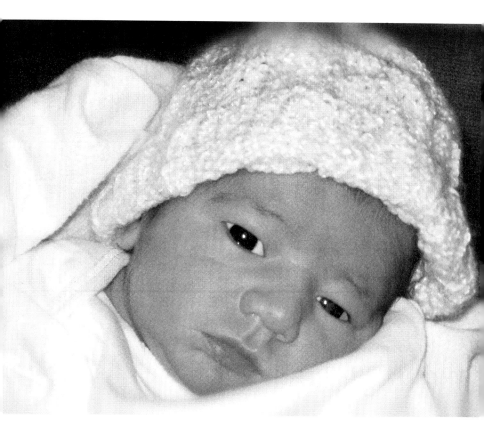

You can't spoil a baby.

*They're only young once,
and it goes by so fast.*

*Expect the unexpected.
You never know what you'll see
or hear; what they'll do or say.*

Every stage is as good as the next, and as the last.

Write down everything the baby does that's exciting or funny or noteworthy; even if it's on scraps of paper. You won't remember anything otherwise. Date them and save them.

All babies are unique. Never compare your child's milestones to another. Someone will always sleep through the night, crawl, stand, and walk before and after your child.

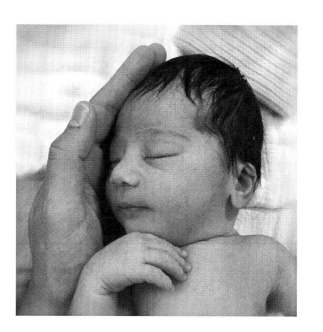

Babies triple their size in the first twelve months. It is the only year that there is such a dramatic change from beginning to end.

Take a photo of your baby each month on the day of their birthday. You'll be amazed at the changes by the end of the twelfth month.

The first birthday and each thereafter is as much a celebration of your success as anything else for your baby.

*1.73 x height at age 3 =
estimated adult height.*

Trust your instincts. If something doesn't seem right, it usually isn't. And, if it ends up that everything is fine, then you're better to be safe than sorry.

*Never feel embarrassed to call the doctor.
That's what they get paid for.*

If something's going to happen, it'll always be on a night, a weekend, a major holiday, during a vacation or a natural disaster.

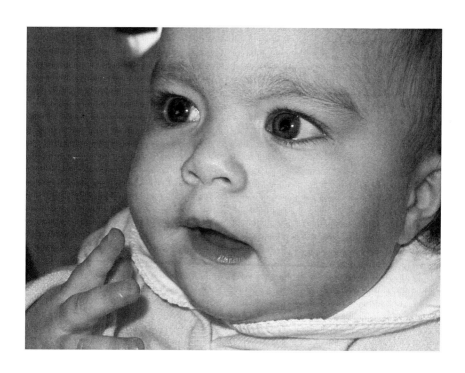

*Pink eye is often accompanied
by an ear infection.*

*Choose a pediatrician close to home.
When they say, "Can you be here in ten
minutes?" you want to be able to say yes.*

*It takes one day to form a bad habit
and three days to break it.*

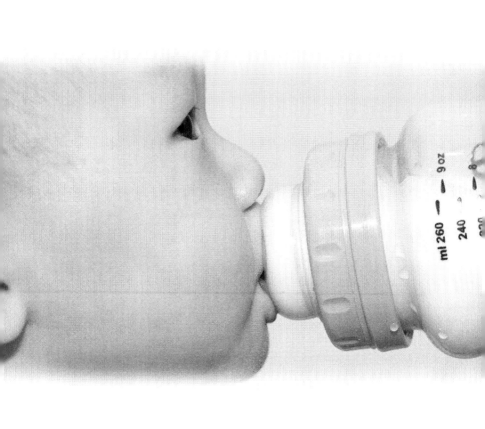

Formula scoops make perfect coffee scoops, so save at least one.

*If it's blue when it goes in,
it's blue when it comes out.*

*As toddlers, three errands in a row
is the limit before a meltdown.*

Tired and hungry are the biggest meltdown triggers, both for the adults and the kids.

Don't allow them to do any behavior once that you don't want them to do a million times.

Once you find something that works, be very consistent. Do it the same way or say it the same way, every time, over and over.

Remember that every baby is an individual. What worked for one may not work for another.

Don't be afraid to say no to your child, firmly and often. The more you say it, the more they will be used to hearing it.

*Every no will make a future yes
that much sweeter to hear.*

*Don't sweat the small stuff.
You'll be very sweaty if you do.*

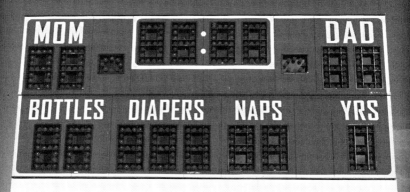

Don't keep score; nobody ever wins.

The best part of experiencing parenthood is being able to relive your favorite childhood experiences. Enjoy every minute.

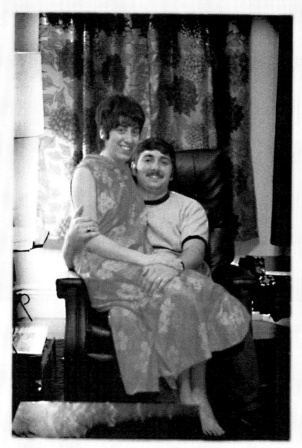

FEB 71

The most interesting thing about parenthood is suddenly realizing what your parents went through physically, emotionally and mentally.

*Always put what's best for your baby first,
even if it's not what's best for you,
or for someone else involved.*

Never say never.

Family dinner time is so important, even when they're babies in a highchair.

Although their needs will constantly change, they will never stop needing you.

*Listen to everyone's advice.
Take from it what you want and
recycle the rest. You'll find your
own way soon enough.*

*Regardless of the bumps in the road,
be sure to enjoy the journey*

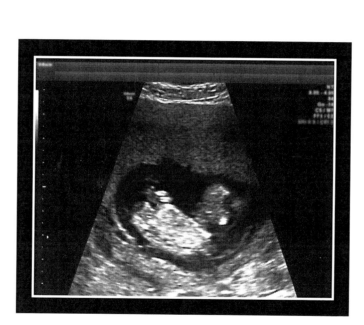

To be continued...

Would you like to be a part of the next *Baby Notes* generation? Submit your photos and/or advice to our website, www.babynotesbook.com to be considered for future *Baby Notes* publications or website postings.

My Own Baby Notes

___

___

___

___

___

___

___

___

___

___

___

My Own Baby Notes

___

___

___

___

___

___

___

___

___

___

___

My Own Baby Notes

___

___

___

___

___

___

___

___

___

___

___

My Own Baby Notes

_____

_____

_____

_____

_____

_____

_____

_____

_____

_____

_____

My Own Baby Notes

_____

_____

_____

_____

_____

_____

_____

_____

_____

_____

_____

The Cowart Family

Don

Jennifer

Caroline

Elizabeth

Alexandra

About the Author

Jennifer Cowart is a wife and the mother of three daughters. She has a degree in Elementary Education and is a freelance writer and photographer. She is the recipient of a New England Press Association award for her education reporting and a Rhode Island Press Association Award for her environmental reporting. She lives with her family in Cranston, Rhode Island.